? Essential Question
What can animals in stories teach us?

The Cat
and the Mice

by Ann Weil

illustrated by Roberta Collier-Morales

Cats are fond of mice. They think mice are delicious! They feast on mice.

They look for mice all day. If cats spot mice, they chase them. It is just what cats do.

Every day, Cat would chase and snatch another mouse. So the mice did something remarkable.

They had a meeting.

"What can we do about
this brute?"

"Be more careful!" said one.

"Make a trap!" said another.

"I believe I know," said an old mouse. "We need to outsmart the cat."

"Use a bell. Put it on the cat's neck. Then we can hear it coming."

STOP AND CHECK

What did the cat do to the mice?

7

"We will have time to run."

"We will have time to hide."

"The bell will save us!"
Now the mice were cheerful.

They had solved the problem,
or so they thought.

Then one mouse asked,
"Who will put the bell on
the cat?"

The mice looked at the old mouse. It was his idea.

What happened after the old mouse shared his idea?

"Not I," he said. "That is a job for a younger mouse."

But none of them would do it.

STOP AND CHECK

What new problem do the mice have?

14

Fables are stories with lessons. The lesson here is: "Easier said than done."

Respond to Reading

Summarize

Use important details to summarize the story.

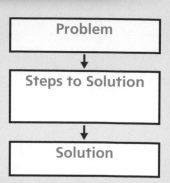

Text Evidence

1. How do you know that *The Cat and the Mice* story is a fable? Genre

2. What problem do the mice have at the beginning of the story? Problem and Solution

3. What does *careful* on page 5 mean? Use the suffix. Suffixes

4. Write about how the mice tried to solve the problem.

Write About Reading

Compare Texts
Read another animal story that can teach a lesson.

Beware of Tiger!

There was a tiger.
It ate other animals.
That's what tigers do.
"If we heard it coming,
we could run away,"
said Deer.

Illustration: Akemi Gutierrez

"I have an idea," said Pig. "Tie a rattle around Tiger's neck!"

Deer agreed. He made the rattle. He found a vine. He gave these to Pig. "Put it on Tiger," said Deer.

"No!" said Pig. "Tiger will eat me!" Something moved in the bushes. Pig and Deer ran away. The lesson is: It is one thing to have an idea, and another to carry it out.

Illustration: Akemi Gutierrez

Make Connections

What did the animals in this story teach you? **Essential Question**

How are they like the mice? **Text To Text**

Focus on
Literary Elements

Dialogue Dialogue is what the characters in a story say.

What to Look For As you read a story, look for quotation marks. They show where dialogue begins and ends. Look at this example from the story:

"No!" said Pig.

Your Turn

Write three sentences of dialogue for an animal story. Use quotation marks around the words each character says.